French
Opera Arias

for

Soprano

and

Orchestra

4070

SUGGESTIONS FOR USING THIS MMO EDITION

WE HAVE TRIED to create a product that will provide you an easy way to learn and perform a concerto with a full orchestra in the comfort of your own home. Because it involves a fixed orchestral performance, there is an inherent lack of flexibility in tempo and cadenza length. The following MMO features and techniques will reduce these inflexibilities and help you maximize the effectiveness of the MMO practice and performance system:

Where the soloist begins a movement *solo*, we have provided an introductory measure with subtle taps inserted at the actual tempo before the soloist's entrance.

Regarding tempi: we have observed generally accepted tempi, but some may wish to perform at a different tempo, or to slow down or speed up the accompaniment for practice purposes. You can purchase from MMO (or from other audio and electronics dealers) specialized CD players which allow variable speed while maintaining proper pitch. This is an indispensable tool for the serious musician and you may wish to look into purchasing this useful piece of equipment for full enjoyment of all your MMO editions.

We want to provide you with the most useful practice and performance accompaniments possible. If you have any suggestions for improving the MMO system, please feel free to contact us. You can reach us by e-mail at mmomusicgroup@musicminusone.com.

Music Minus One

4070

FRENCH
OPERA ARIAS
FOR
SOPRANO AND ORCHESTRA

A Note on the Arias

Lakmé
by Léo Delibes
Scene et Legende de la Fille du Paria
(*"The Bell Song"*)
sung by Lakmé

It was with the 1883 premiere of *Lakmé* that Léo Delibes (1836-1891), the 47-year-old French composer of ballets, fulfilled his longtime ambition to compose a serious opera. That *Lakmé's* lasting success is almost entirely due to Delibes' triumph at composing for the coloratura voice goes without question. The title rôle has long been a showcase for the most ambitious of sopranos—and doubtless will remain so. Luisa Tetrazzini, Adelina Patti and Lily Pons are but a few of the great names of the past who enhanced their reputations in singing Lakmé's beautifully melodic arias.

Delibes took his cue for this opera from the nineteenth-century French obsession with the Middle East and the Orient. Located in British India, the plot concerns the hatred Brahmin priests hold for their British invaders, who have forbidden these highest-cast Indians from practicing their ancient religion.

It is in Act II that Lakmé has been ordered by her father, an angry Brahmin priest, to sing the *Scene et Legende de la Fille du Paria* (also known as *the Bell Song*), in order to draw out and identify two British officers who earlier violated sacred Indian ground.

☙❧

Carmen
by Georges Bizet
"C'est des contrebandiers ... Je dis, que rien"
sung by Micaela

Is *Carmen* the greatest of all operas? It certainly is one of the most performed, and without question it resides firmly among the five most popular ever composed. But is it indeed *the greatest?* Questions of this sort are amusing to pose and ponder, but are, due to the relativity of tastes, ultimately futile. The closest we can come to answering that impossible question is that in terms of the sheer "hum-ablity" of its melodies, *Carmen* has all other operas beat, hands down.

What is often forgotten today is that upon its premiere in Paris in 1875, *Carmen* was considered a failure. The early death of its composer George Bizet (1838-1875) on the night of its thirty-third performance was most likely exacerbated by his despair at his masterpiece's negative reception. After fifty performances at the *Opera-Comique* during its first two seasons, *Carmen* wasn't performed in Paris for another seven years—during which time it won great acclaim across Europe and beyond. Upon its return to Paris in 1883, *Carmen* was hailed as a world-wide triumph and the Parisian audiences conveniently forgot their initial reaction; but unfortunately Bizet was no longer alive to forgive them for their fickle tastes.

In Act III, Micaela is led by a guide to the mountain encampment temporarily deserted by Carmen and José. Still in love with José despite his passion for Carmen, Micaela has come here to tell Jose that his mother is dying. Her very lovely aria *"C'est des contrebandiers...Je dis, que rien"* is essentially a prayer in which she asks for strength.

☙❧

Roméo et Juliet
by Charles Gounod
"Ah! Je veux vivre"
sung by Juliette

The most spectacular initial operatic success of Charles Gounod (1818-1893) was *Roméo et Juliet.* This glory was enhanced in no small way due to its premiering during the *Exposition Universelle* of 1867, when Paris was invaded by hordes of visitors from across France and around the world. A new opera by Gounod, the composer of the immensely popular *Faust* (1859), was bound to draw packed houses every night, and it did just that—helping to rapidly spread its fame abroad.

There's good reason for the opera's mass appeal: not only does it possess a beloved and durable story, but for it Gounod composed some of his most magical melodies. To quote George Bernard Shaw, *Roméo et Juliet* radiates a "...spell of the heavenly melody...the exquisite orchestral web of sound colours...." In artistry and beauty, Gounod's *Roméo et Juliet* stands alongside those other masterful musical adaptations of the same story—Prokofiev's ballet, Tchaikovsky's overture, Berlioz's dramatic symphony, as well as Bernstein's modern-day version, *West Side Story.*

In Act I, a masked ball is underway at the Capulet residence. Montague intruders enter disguised behind masks, Roméo among them. He catches sight of Juliet in the distance and falls instantly in love, after which Juliet enters with her nurse, Gertrude. Not knowing that she herself is about to fall in love with Roméo, Juliet sings *"Je Veux vivre"* as a lighthearted statement that she is disinterested in ever marrying.

⚜

MIGNON
by Ambroise Thomas
Polonaise of Philine
sung by Philine

Ambroise Thomas (1811-1896) never stood among the top echelon of opera composers, but in his day he had quite a measure of success. Almost all of his works were performed in Paris at the Opera-Comique, and that theatre inevitably set the predominantly lightweight tone of his works, most of which have not survived the ultimate test of time. A comment from Emmanuel Chabrier adequately sums up the late-nineteenth-century French attitude regarding this composer, about there being "three kinds of music—good, bad and Ambroise Thomas."

Two of his operas, however, do indeed hold up and will no doubt continue to keep his name in the repertoire as long as opera is performed: *Mignon* (premiered in Paris in 1866) and *Hamlet* (premiered in Paris 1868). Both were resounding successes in their day, and deservedly so, for both are rich in melody and plot. That both are based on great stories helps to explain why these are the only works of Thomas which have endured. *Hamlet,* of course, is based on Shakespeare's play; while *Mignon* is based on Goethe's classic novel, *Wilhelm Meister.*

In Act II, Scene 2 of *Mignon,* in the castle gardens, Mignon despairingly wants to drown herself, but Lothario prevents her from doing so; both then flee at the sound of singing coming from inside the castle. Philine excitedly enters the gardens from inside, having just performed the rôle of Titania in *A Midsummer's Night Dream*; she sings the famous *Polonaise of Philine.*

Thomas ingeniously crafts this aria in the form of a *polonaise,* using marvelous effects, dazzling runs and coquettish coloratura. It is the joyous focal point of the finale of Act II, as well as the high-point of the entire opera.

⚜

LES CONTES D'HOFFMAN
by Jacques Offenbach
"Les oiseaux dans la charmille"
(*The Doll's Song*)
sung by Olympia

Unlike the music of any other composer, that of Jacques Offenbach (1819-1880) captures that gay, frivolous atmosphere of Paris during the Second Empire and the early years of the Third Republic. Offenbach achieved this through his numerous light operas known as *opera bouffes*—all wonderfully ironic, silly, and filled with Offenbach's buoyant tunes.

It is ironic then that off all of Offenbach's works, *Les Contes d'Hoffman* should be known today as his most famous opera as well as his most often performed. Despite its lush, lyrical melodies so typical of this composer, it is the least typical work of his entire output. For this, Offenbach was making an attempt at gaining recognition as a serious composer.

And by all accounts he succeeded, for *Les Contes d'Hoffman* is his masterpiece. Which makes for yet another irony, this time one tinged by great tragedy. Offenbach died during rehearsals, leaving it somewhat unfinished (which explains the many differing versions in circulation) and preventing its author from learning that he finally gained entry into the pantheon of serious composers.

In Act II, the poet Hoffman is in love with Olympia, whom he thinks is the daughter of the inventor Spalanzani. It is revealed, however, that she is actually one of Spalanzani's inventions—for Olympia is a mechanical doll. Not knowing this, Hoffman sings of his love for her. And Olympia sings in response the charming aria *"Les oiseaux dans la charmille."*

—*Douglas Scharmann*

Lakmé

Scène et Légende de la Fille du Paria
(The Bell Song)

Léo Delibes

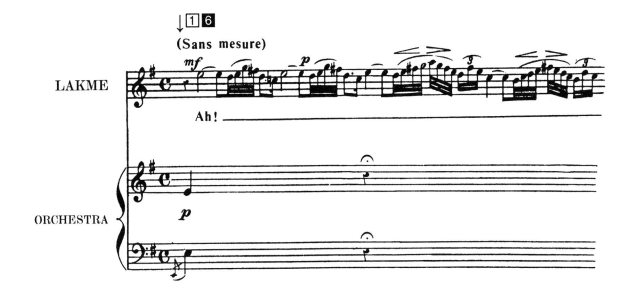

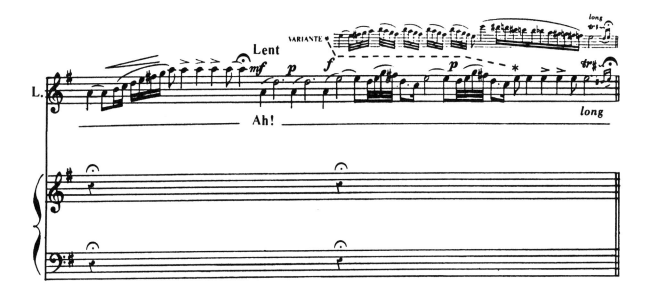

8

CARMEN

"C'est de contrebandiers...Je dis, que rien"

GEORGES BIZET

24

MMO 4070

ROMEO ET JULIETTE
"Ah! Je veux vivre"

CHARLES GOUNOD

Dans ce rê - ve __ qui m'en -

i - vre __ Long - temps en - -cor __

Dou - ce flam - me, __ Je te

gar - de __ dans mon â - me __

Com - - - -meun tré - sor. Cet - te ivres - -se

De jeu-nes- -se Ne dure, hé - las! qu'un jour.

Puis vient l'heu - re Où l'on pleu - re, Le cœur cè - de à l'a-

mour, Et _ le _ bon- -heur _ fuit_

sans_ re - tour._ Ah!

Je veux vi- -vre _ Dans ce

rê- -ve ___ qui m'en- -i- -vre ___

cresc.

Long- -temps en- -cor! Dou- -ce

dim.

p

flam- -me, ___ Je te gar- -de ___

cresc. molto

dans mon â- -me ___ Com- -meun tré-

f

Ah!

cresc.

Dou - ce

flam - - me, Res - - te dans mon â - -

me Com - me un doux tré - sor _____ Long - -

temps en - - cor! _____

MIGNON
Polonaise of Philine

Ambroise Thomas

Moderato tempo di Polocca. (96 = ♩)

PHILINE.

Je_ suis Tita-ni_a la blon _ de, Je_ suis Titani_a fil - le_ de l'air! En ri_ant_ je parcours le mon _ de Plus vi _ ve que_ l'oiseau, plus prompte_ que _____ l'éclair:

Je_ suis Tita_ni_a la blon _ de! Ah! _____

blon _ de Ah!

léger et accentué

La troupe fol _ le des lutins Suit __ Mon char qui vole et dans la nuit Fuit!

Autour de moi toute ma cour, Court __ Chantant le plai _ sir et l'amour.

Je suis Ti _ tà _ ni _ a fil _ _ _ le _ de

l'air: Ah! ah! _____ ah!

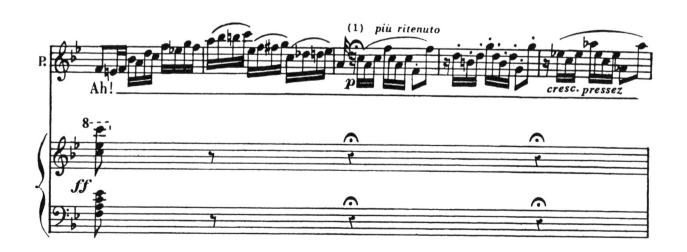

Ah! _____ (1) *più ritenuto* *cresc. pressez*

LES CONTES D'HOFFMAN

"Les oiseaux dans la charmille"

JACQUES OFFENBACH

a,_____ d'O-lym-pi - a! Ah!_____ ah!_____

ah!_____ ah!_____ ah!_____

OLYMPIA.

Tout ce qui chan-te et ré - son - - - - - - - ne Et sou - pi - re, tour à tour,_____ É - meut son cœur qui fris - son - ne, É - meut son cœur qui fris -

OPERA with ORCHESTRA

Music Minus One is proud to present the finest arias in the operatic repertoire—now available with full orchestral accompaniment! We have brought the finest European vocalists and orchestras together to create an unparalleled experience—giving you the opportunity to sing opera the way it was meant to be performed. All titles are now CD+Graphics encoded so you can see the lyrics on your television screen in real-time—and, as always, the full printed vocal score is included as well.

Soprano

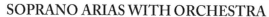

SOPRANO ARIAS WITH ORCHESTRA
Zvetelina Maldjanska – Vidin Philharmonic/Todorov   MMO CDG 4052
Puccini – La Bohème *Mi chiamano Mimi (Mimi)*; Mozart – Die Zauberflöte *Ach, ich fühl's*; Verdi – I Vespri Siciliani *Siciliana d'Elena*; Bizet – Les Pêcheurs de Perles *Me voilà seule dans la nuit*; Meyerbeer – Dinorah *Ombre légère qui suis mes pas (Shadow song) (Dinorah)*

SOPRANO ARIAS WITH ORCHESTRA
Ljudmila Gerova – Festival Orchestra of Bulgaria/Todorov   MMO CDG 4054
W.A. Mozart - Recitative and Aria *Ergo Interest, an quis…Quære Superna*, KV. 143; Mozart - Le Nozze di Figaro *Venite, inginocchiatevi (Susanna)*; Mozart – Le Nozze di Figaro *Giunse alfin il momento…Deh Vieni, non tardar (Susanna)*; C.M. v.Weber – Der Freischütz *Und ob die Wolke sie verhülle*; Puccini – Tosca *Vissi d'arte, vissi d'amore*

BELLINI OPERA SCENES AND ARIAS FOR SOPRANO AND ORCHESTRA
Zvetelina Maldjanska – Plovdiv Philharmonic/Todorov   MMO CDG 4063
Norma *Casta diva…Fine al rito…Ah! bello a mi ritorna (Norma)*; I Puritani *Qui la voce sua soave…Vien, diletto (Elvira)*.

LA SONNAMBULA: SCENES AND ARIAS FOR SOPRANO AND ORCHESTRA
Zvetelina Maldjanska – Plovdiv Philharmonic/Todorov   MMO CDG 4064
Care compagne…A te, diletta, tenera madre…Come per me sereno..Sovra il sen (Amina); *Ah! Se una volta sola…Ah! non credea mirarti…Ah! Non giunge (Amina)*

DONIZETTI SOPRANO SCENES & ARIAS WITH ORCHESTRA
Zvetelina Maldjanska – Plovdiv Philharmonic/Todorov   MMO CDG 4058
Don Pasquale – Act I, Scene 4 *Quel guardo il cavaliere…So anch'io la virtù magica (Norina)*; Lucia di Lammermoor – Act I, Scene 2: *Quella fonte… – Regnava nel silenzio – Quando rapito in estasi (Lucia)*; Lucia di Lammermoor – Act II, Scene 5 *Il dolce suono – Ardon gl'Incensi – Alfin son tua – spargi d'amaro pianto (Lucia)*

MOZART OPERA ARIAS FOR SOPRANO AND ORCHESTRA
Zvetelina Maldjanska – Plovdiv Philharmonic/Todorov   MMO CDG 4060
Don Giovanni *In quali eccessi, o Numi…Mi tradì quell' alma ingrata (Donna Elvira)*; Die Zauberflöte *Ach, ich fühl's, es ist verschwunden (Pamina)*; Le Nozze di Figaro *E Susanna non vien!…Dove sono I bei momenti (Contessa)*; Le Nozze di Figaro *Giunse alfin il momento…Deh Vieni, non tardar (Susanna)*; Die Entführung aus dem Serail *Martern aller Arten (Constanze)*

MOZART OPERA ARIAS FOR SOPRANO AND ORCHESTRA, VOLUME II
Snejana Dramtcheva - Plovdiv Philharmonic/Todorov   MMO CDG 4065
Die Zauberflöte *O zitt're nicht, mein lieber Sohn…Zum Leiden bin ich auserkoren (Queen of the Night)*; Die Entführung aus dem Serail *Durch Zärtlichkeit und Schmeicheln (Blonde)*; Die Entführung aus dem Serail *Welche Wonne, welche Lust herrscht nun mehr in meiner Brust (Blonde)*; Così fan tutte *Una donna a quindici anni (Despina)*; Don Giovanni *Batti, batti, o bel Masetto (Zerlina)*; Don Giovanni *Vedrai, carino, se sei buonino (Zerlina)*

PUCCINI SOPRANO ARIAS WITH ORCHESTRA
Zvetelina Maldjanska – Plovdiv Philharmonic Orchestra/Todorov   MMO CDG 4053
La Bohème *Mi chiamano Mimi (Mimi)*; La Bohème *Quando me'n vo' soletta la via" (Musetta)*; La Bohème *Donde lieta (Mimi)*; Gianni Schicchi – *O mio babbino caro (Lauretta)*; Turanodot *Signore, ascolta! (Liù)*; Turandot *Tu che di gel sei cinta (Liù)*

VERDI SOPRANO OPERA ARIAS WITH ORCHESTRA
Zvetelina Maldjanska – Plovdiv Philharmonic/Todorov   MMO CDG 4059
La Traviata *È strano! È strano!...Ah fors'è lui che l'anima solinga ne' tumulti...Follie! Sempre libera* (*Violetta*); I Vespri Siciliani (*Siciliana d'Elena*) *Mercè, dilette amiche (Elena)*; Falstaff *Sul fil d'un soffio etesio (Nannetta)*; Otello *Piangea cantando (The Willow Song) (Desdemona)*; Rigoletto *Caro nome (Gilda)*; La Traviata – Scene *Attendo, attendo...* and aria *Addio del passato (Violetta)*

Mezzo-Soprano

VERDI MEZZO-SOPRANO ARIAS WITH ORCHESTRA
Ivanka Ninova – Festival Orchestra of Bulgaria/Todorov   MMO CDG 4055
Il Trovatore *Condotta ell'era in ceppi (Azucena)*; Il Trovatore *Stride la vampa! (Azucena)*; Don Carlo *O don fatale (Eboli)*; Don Carlo *Nei giardin del bello (Eboli)*; Nabucco *Oh, dischiuso, è il firmamento (Fenena)*

FRENCH & ITALIAN OPERA ARIAS FOR MEZZO-SOPRANO AND ORCHESTRA
Ivanka Ninova – Plovdiv Philharmonic/Todorov   MMO CDG 4062
Bizet – Carmen *L'amour est un oiseau rebelle (La Havanaise) (Carmen)*; Saint-Saëns – Samson et Dalila *Samson, recherchant ma présence (Dalila)*; Cilea – Adriana Lecouvreur *Acerba volutta...Ognieco, ogni ombra...O vagabonda stella d'Oriente (La Principessa)*; Ponchielli – La Gioconda *Voce di donna o d'angelo (Cieca)*; Mascagni – Cavalleria Rusticana Voi lo sapete, o mama (*Santuzza*); Donizetti – La Favorita *Fia dunque vero? (Leonora)*

Tenor

ITALIAN TENOR ARIAS WITH ORCHESTRA
Kamen Tchanev – Plovdiv Philharmonic/Todorov   MMO CDG 4057
Puccini – La Bohème *Che gelida manina (Rodolfo)*; Puccini – Tosca *Recondita armonia (Cavaradossi)*; Donizetti – L'Elisir d'Amore *Una furtiva lagrima (Nemorino)*; Verdi – Rigoletto *La donna è mobile (Duca)*; Verdi – La Traviata scene and aria: *Lunge da Lei...De' miei bollenti spiriti (Alfredo)*

PUCCINI ARIAS FOR TENOR AND ORCHESTRA
Vesselin Hristov – Plovdiv Philharmonic Orchestra/Todorov   MMO CDG 4061
Turandot *Nessun dorma! (Calaf)*; Turandot *Non piangere, Liù! (Il Principe)*; Tosca *Recondita armonia (Cavaradossi)*; Tosca E lucevan le stel*le (Cavaradossi)*; Madama Butterfly Addio, Fiorito asil (Pinkerton); *Manon Lescaut Donna non vidi* mai simile *a questa! (Des Grieux)*; La Bohème *Che gelida manina (Rodolfo)*

Bass-Baritone

BASS-BARITONE ARIAS WITH ORCHESTRA
Ivaylo Djourov – Festival Orchestra of Bulgaria/Todorov   MMO CDG 4056
Mozart – Le Nozze di Figaro *Vedrò mentr'io sospiro (Il Conte)*; Mozart – Le Nozze di Figaro *Se vuol ballare, signor contino (Figaro)*; Rossini – Il Barbiere di Siviglia *La callunia è un venticello (Basilio)*; Verdi – Simon Boccanegra *Il lacerato spirito (Fiesco)*; Puccini – La Bohème *Vecchia zimarra (Colline)*

The John Wustman Series of Vocal Recordings

In a field dominated by the vocal soloist, John Wustman is one of the few accompanists in this country who has achieved renown and critical acclaim in this most challenging of art forms. Mr. Wustman has developed that rare quality of bringing a strength and character to his accompaniments which create a true collaboration between the singer and the pianist. And this is as it should be, for in the art song especially the piano part is not mere rhythmic and tonal background, but an integral part of the composer's intent and creation. Thus, on these recordings, Mr. Wustman provides not only the necessary accompaniment but also through his artistry, stylistic and interpretive suggestion for the study of the music.

Among the many artists he has accompanied in past years are Montserrat Caballe, Regine Crespin, Nicolai Gedda, Anna Moffo, Birgit Nilsson, Jan Peerce, Roberta Peters, Elisabeth Schwarzkopf, Renata Scotto and William Warfield.

Mr. Wustman has become known to millions of television viewers as the accompanist to Luciano Pavarotti in his many appearances in that medium.

Lieder

BRAHMS GERMAN LIEDER for High Voice ....MMO CD 4005
SCHUBERT GERMAN LIEDER for High Voice, Vol. 1 ....MMO CD 4001
SCHUBERT GERMAN LIEDER for High Voice, Vol. 2 ....MMO CD 4003
SCHUMANN GERMAN LIEDER for High Voice ....MMO CD 4024
STRAUSS GERMAN LIEDER for High Voice ....MMO CD 4022
WOLF GERMAN LIEDER for High Voice ....MMO CD 4020
17th/18th CENT. ITALIAN SONGS for High Voice, Vol. 1 ......MMO CD 4011
17th/18th CENT. ITALIAN SONGS for High Voice, Vol. 2 ......MMO CD 4013
EVERYBODY'S FAVORITE SONGS for High Voice, Vol. 1 ...MMO CD 4007
EVERYBODY'S FAVORITE SONGS for High Voice, Vol. 2 ...MMO CD 4009

BRAHMS GERMAN LIEDER for Low Voice ....MMO CD 4006
SCHUBERT GERMAN LIEDER for Low Voice, Vol. 1 ....MMO CD 4002
SCHUBERT GERMAN LIEDER for Low Voice, Vol. 2 ....MMO CD 4004
SCHUMANN GERMAN LIEDER for Low Voice ....MMO CD 4025
STRAUSS GERMAN LIEDER for Low Voice ....MMO CD 4023
WOLF GERMAN LIEDER for Low Voice ....MMO CD 4021
17th/18th CENT. ITALIAN SONGS for Low Voice, Vol. 1 ....MMO CD 4012
17th/18th CENT. ITALIAN SONGS for Low Voice, Vol. 2 ....MMO CD 4014
EVERYBODY'S FAVORITE SONGS for Low Voice, Vol. 1 ....MMO CD 4008
EVERYBODY'S FAVORITE SONGS for Low Voice, Vol. 2 ....MMO CD 4010

Arias

FAMOUS SOPRANO ARIAS ....MMO CD 4015
MOZART ARIAS FOR SOPRANO ....MMO CD 4026
VERDI ARIAS FOR SOPRANO ....MMO CD 4027
ITALIAN ARIAS FOR SOPRANO ....MMO CD 4028
FRENCH ARIAS FOR SOPRANO ....MMO CD 4029
ORATORIO ARIAS FOR SOPRANO ....MMO CD 4030

FAMOUS MEZZO-SOPRANO ARIAS ....MMO CD 4016

ORATORIO ARIAS FOR ALTO ....MMO CD 4031

FAMOUS TENOR ARIAS ....MMO CD 4017
ORATORIO ARIAS FOR TENOR ....MMO CD 4032

FAMOUS BARITONE ARIAS ....MMO CD 4018

FAMOUS BASS ARIAS ....MMO CD 4019
ORATORIO ARIAS FOR BASS ....MMO CD 4033

Laureate Series Contest Solos

BEGINNING SOPRANO SOLOS KATE HURNEY/BRUCE EBERLE ....MMO CD 4041
INTERMEDIATE SOPRANO SOLOS KATE HURNEY/BRUCE EBERLE ....MMO CD 4042

BEGINNING MEZZO-SOPRANO SOLOS FAY KITTELSON/RICHARD FOSTER ....MMO CD 4043
INTERMEDIATE MEZZO-SOPRANO SOLOS FAY KITTELSON/RICHARD FOSTER ......MMO CD 4044
ADVANCED MEZZO-SOPRANO SOLOS FAY KITTELSON/RICHARD FOSTER.............MMO CD 4045

BEGINNING CONTRALTO SOLOS CARLINE RAY/BRUCE EBERLE ....MMO CD 4046

BEGINNING TENOR SOLOS GEORGE SHIRLEY/WAYNE SANDERS................................MMO CD 4047
INTERMEDIATE TENOR SOLOS GEORGE SHIRLEY/WAYNE SANDERS........................MMO CD 4048
ADVANCED TENOR SOLOS GEORGE SHIRLEY/WAYNE SANDERS................................MMO CD 4049

TWELVE CLASSIC VOCAL STANDARDS, VOL.1 ....MMO CD 4050
TWELVE CLASSIC VOCAL STANDARDS, VOL.2 ....MMO CD 4051

AVAILABLE FROM FINE MUSIC AND RECORD DEALERS
OR VISIT US AT WWW.MUSICMINUSONE.COM
TO ORDER BY PHONE CALL 1-800-669-7464 (U.S.) • 914-592-1188 (INT'L)

MUSIC MINUS ONE
50 Executive Boulevard
Elmsford, New York 10523-1325
800-669-7464 (U.S.)/914-592-1188 (International)

www.musicminusone.com
e-mail: mmogroup@musicminusone.com

MMO 4070

Printed in Canada